About the Author

Born and raised in a London suburb during the early 1930s, he followed a childhood ambition by joining the RAF as a Boy Entrant in 1947. Following graduation he served almost 30 years working on three continents, and various places around Europe and the Mediterranean. Retiring as a commissioned Engineer Officer in 1976, he started a new career as a Customs Officer, serving at Dover, one of the busiest ports in Europe. Retiring again in 1991, he followed a life-long interest in WW1, and obtained occasional work as a tour guide around the battle fields of WW1. Other interests, in family history and painting, led to the writing of two books on the family history, never published but widely circulated within the family. Bill is now a resident in Norfolk, enjoying life!

William Thomas Littler

LETTERS FROM A POSTMAN

AUSTIN MACAULEY PUBLISHERS™
LONDON • CAMBRIDGE • NEW YORK • SHARJAH

A CIP catalogue record for this title is available from the British Library.

ISBN 9781398407992 (Paperback)
ISBN 9781398408005 (ePub e-book)

www.austinmacauley.com

First Published (2021)
Austin Macauley Publishers Ltd
25 Canada Square
Canary Wharf
London
E14 5LQ

Acknowledgements

I would like to express my gratitude to my daughter-in-law, Louise, and her mother, who are the custodians of the letters, postcards, photographs etc, that appear in this book. They originally showed me the letters knowing of my interest in WW1. A later suggestion that I might like to sort them out and edit them, led directly to this book.

Horace Surtees was born on 10 March 1887, the seventh child of William and Louisa Surtees. The elder children were William, Emily, Arthur, Conyers, Thomas and May (twins). After Horace came George, Alice and finally Dorothy who was to die in the Spanish flu epidemic, aged 10 years.

They were a happy family, of modest but adequate means, who lived a happy life in the Fulham district of London.

When it came time to settle on a career, Horace found a job as a postman for which a high degree of reliability and honesty was required. Sometime around 1904/05, Horace met a young lady named Maggie Young. She was in domestic service and they became friends. Maggie's employment was to take her abroad to Belgium for a time but the young people carried on their courtship, for that is what it had become, by mail. Several picture postcards survive, showing an increasing familiarity and strong bonds developing between them. (Plate 1 and 2). On Maggie's return to England, they continued to meet and occasionally to correspond by post (Plate 3 and 4). Remember, this was in the days when it was possible to post a letter in the morning and have it delivered by midday. Eventually, these young people were to marry in 1911. Their daughter, known to all as 'young Maggie', was born in 1912. As with most babies, she was her mother's pride and joy, and her father's favourite and delight. The other members of the family, her grandparents, uncles and aunts loved her almost as much and she was a firm favourite of everyone.

In 1914, the Great War began which was to have such a devastating effect on everyone. At first, the young Surtees family were not very involved apart from the normal problems of food shortages and the sudden disappearance of many young men into the Army or Navy. Elder brothers William, Arthur and Conyer led the way. Then, on 8 December 1915, Horace felt it was time for him to do his bit and at the age of 28, he volunteered for the Army. His enlistment papers give brief details showing that Horace was 5 feet 5 inches tall, dark-brown haired, blue eyed and of fresh complexion. His occupation shown as postman (Staff). He was attested for the 6th London Regiment. Little more is known of his life as a soldier, until 27 August 1916, when Horace sends a picture postcard to Maggie from the training camp at Fovant on Salisbury Plain (Plate 5). This is in the form of a typically martial poem, showing the eagerness of the trainees to get to grips with the enemy who will quail and run when confronted with "the boys from Fovant". As the initial enlistment papers (Plate 6) indicate, Horace was not paid as a soldier until 8 June 1916. It is possible that he was not called forward to join his new regiment until that time and that Fovant Camp was his first military unit.

The only other surviving piece of mail from that time is a postcard, with a picture of what seems to be a cross-channel ferry (Plate 7). Dated 11 October 1916. It carries the somewhat terse message, "Dear M, Sunday, arrived safe somewhere in France. Letter following." That being the first indication that rifleman H. Surtees has gone off to war.

Plate 1. Postcard from Maggie, whilst employed in Belgium.

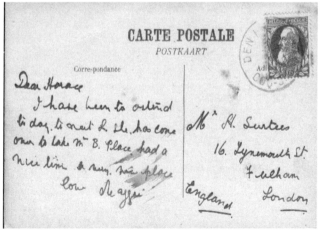

Plate 2. Message on reverse of Plate 1.

From here on, however, there begins a wonderful series of letters sent by Horace to his dear wife and daughter. In them, he gives a dramatic picture of the life of the ordinary soldier at that time. His hopes and fears and his longings for the things he misses most. In transcribing these letters, no attempt has been made to change style or grammar. Spelling is usually correct and only occasionally has it been necessary to make changes. So, here commences a private look into the life of reluctant soldier Horace Surtees, revealed in a remarkable collection of letters from a postman.

****

Monday, 12 October 1916. 6125 Rifleman H. Surtees
6th London Regiment
15 Camp 8th Infantry Base
Le Havre, FRANCE

My Dearest Darling Maggie,

Just a line to let you know I arrived safe and sound, sent you postcard yesterday (Plate 7), don't destroy it, you can guess what it is. Had rotten rough passage over, shall not forget it in a hurry. Never felt so bad in my life before. Lost nearly all my insides, B------ it was quite a sight to see the fellows sick and bad. Anyhow, I fully recovered from that sickness now. My feet are a treat now. I expect it was that continuous walking for a long time from Wilton from 6 am to 11 am. Anyhow, I wouldn't give way. I greatly admired your pluck for keeping up your spirits at the last. Many a woman would have broke down long before. The fellows near me were surprised at your spirits, even I was. Hoping you arrived home safe from your short holiday. The watch is going great. Having some nice weather now. Did you have enough money for your keep? Don't forget whatever your expenses were let me know. Put it down to my account. Will pay you when the war is over. Have you received my photo from Mrs Reading yet? When you see the old man, ask him if he knows Bill Reading, ex cabman. That's her father. He spotted my face in photo after she said, "That's Surtees." Rather funny how you meet people. He had letter from her on Friday morning. Never know who you are speaking to in our days. Hoping you are in best of health also little Maggie. Tell her I will soon be home again. Also tell her I am somewhere in France. Well, my dear, cannot tell you much news, will only be blacked over if I do,

10

so must close hoping you and little Maggie are first rate, with very best love and kisses, from your loving Husband, Horace.

Written in pencil, as all the letters are, this was written on Y.M.C.A headed paper, with the words "On Active Service with The British Expeditionary Force" in bold type at the top.

Plate 3. Posted at 10:30 am

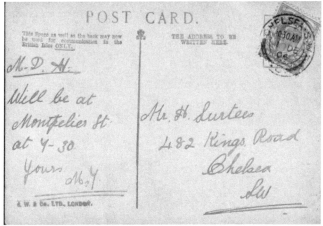

Plate 4. Received by 5:30 pm

So, Horace has begun his war. The crossing to France was very rough, as so many of them seemed to be and most of the soldiers appeared to have suffered from the effects.

From the words in the letter, is seems that Maggie had managed to travel down to the camp at Fovant and spend a brief spell with Horace, which necessitated him walking to and from the camp over quite a large distance. However, his feet have now recovered and he has time to admire Maggie's going away present, a new watch.

He wrote next on Thursday, 12 October.

Still at the Base Camp.

My dearest Darling Maggie,

Just a line telling you that I am in the best of health and spirits, also merry and bright. Hoping you and little Maggie are the same. Having some awful weather now, those heavy showers that damn near drowns one. Our tent is not washed away yet. Lucky for us, it's pretty well dry. Hard job at night to sleep when pouring down with rain. Make hell of a row on tent. Just as though someone throwing stones on it. Also, hard job to keep on our feet. This camp on a slope, which make to walk in the dark awkward. Last night had the pleasure of slipping over twice in the dark. You can guess what a nice state I was in. Don't care to tell you the words I used. Wishing I and the army was elsewhere. Had a nice route march today around some of the French villages, in the mud. Nice heavy showers in between. Rather cramped houses we passed, wouldn't give our rabbit room in them. Something after the style of houses you told me you saw in Belgium. Sending little Maggie Postcard (Plate 8 and 9). You will notice on the birds that there are allied flags worked on them, very pretty. Take care of them, cost 50 centimes, some of them 60, which is 5d and 6d in English money. I thought of having them in a frame someday, will make a nice picture. Sending you a special one next time I write. Going to send PC to Mrs Glasson tonight. Just had letter from Mother telling me George is in France. Also, Con has total exemption, lucky chap. She considers that photo of the four are great (Plate 9). No doubt you think the same, anyhow think they are very good. Us four are highly pleased with them. Will you send me a common fag case as carrying them in our pockets they get broken and are no use. Also, a pocketbook, one I can keep letters in and items. Only get a cheap one. Tried and cannot get one here. Don't pay a lot for them. Pack them well or else they might be missing. Well, my dearest, have no more news for you so must close with very best love to you and little Maggie. Hoping this will find you both in the pink. From your loving husband, Horace.

Horace is now meeting the rigours of tented accommodation in wet weather and the difficulties of walking and sleeping. Interestingly, the Army treatment for lack of sleep seems to be a long route march in the rain. Toughening them up perhaps? For the first, time Horace mentions the postcards which he was to send regularly throughout his time in France. These are the heavily embroidered cards, with patriotic scenes and themes, or Regimental badges sewn in full colour. Fortunately, Maggie heeded his request to save them and a selection is featured in this anthology.

The next letter, still from the base camp at Le Havre, is dated Saturday, 14 October 1916.

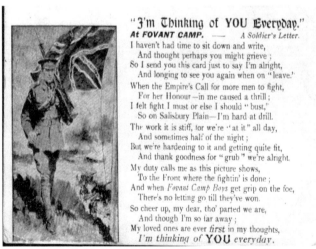

Plate 6. From our gallant soldier in training.

My Dearest darling Maggie,

Thanks for the kind letter received this evening, dated Thursday, 12 October. Glad to hear you received them safe and that you and little Maggie are all right. Will answer your letter further on. Glad to say I am in the best of health and spirits. Still having nice weather. This place of course is much larger than Hurdcott. We are in tents, not so nice as huts but most amusing bedtime (there are 13 of us). When we put our feet down in fact, we are like sardines in a box but still we all sleep well, anyhow I do. Up every morning in the dark at 5 am. Get to bed about 10, so you can guess it don't require a lot of rocking. Nice bathhouse here, plenty of hot water, also proper place to wash our clothes. Also, hot water far better than Hurdcott. As regards that, French money and notes are hard to pick up but quite understand them now. Seems funny walking on the opposite side of the road. Keep wanting to walk on the left side of road, fancy I'm in England. We managed to get in the same tent, the four of us. Those four you will see in the photo when you see them.

Ran across two fellows I knew. One of them was Pearce, postman at Earls Court. Tells me he saw you one day in Wandsworth Rd, when up. You know him well. I was greatly surprised when I came out of Poison Gas chamber, someone called out "Surtees"; it was him. Cannot mention what regiment he is in. As you know, we have to be careful what we write about. We are not allowed out of camp, which makes it rotten, so in our spare time we walk about the camp. We have plenty of training here, starts from 7:30 in the morning, come back about 4:30, have half hour for lunch and about one and a half for dinner. Take our rations with us. Biscuits and cheese or corn beef and have our dinner and tea together. Cannot tell you much about our food. Will tell you all about it when I come home. Talking about biscuits, always think of the girls when eating them. They are made at McFarlanes. Not so bad. Getting used to them. Have plenty of them here. We have a good training here. Different to what we been having. We do Infantry drill, quite a change from our drilling and it's done by men from the trenches, men that know how things should be done, mostly by Guardsmen. Been through Poison Gas Chamber with gas helmets on, not very pleasant, also tear shell trench Tear gas smells all the world like pineapple. Just like someone pricking one's eyes with pins. We do everything here, trench making, barbwire, bombing, firing, bayoneting etc. Everything that useful to us. Some very nice Officers here, instructors. Had one today telling us for God's sake to keep writing home to our people telling them that we are all right. Told us that we have nothing to worry about, but our people have, wanting and waiting to know if their people are all right in the trenches. I consider him quite right, don't you? Telling us a few yarns, made roars of laughter. Spoke to us like a good father. When having meals here, have to take our hats off and be fully dressed. Don't clean our boots or kit. Can write as many letters and postcards as you like. Letters go out in the mornings and we receive our letters at night, so you can see we only have one post a day. Everybody looking for letters from home. Quite a sight to see us and their faces when no letters for them. YMCA here hell of a job to get served. Very handy, couldn't do without it.

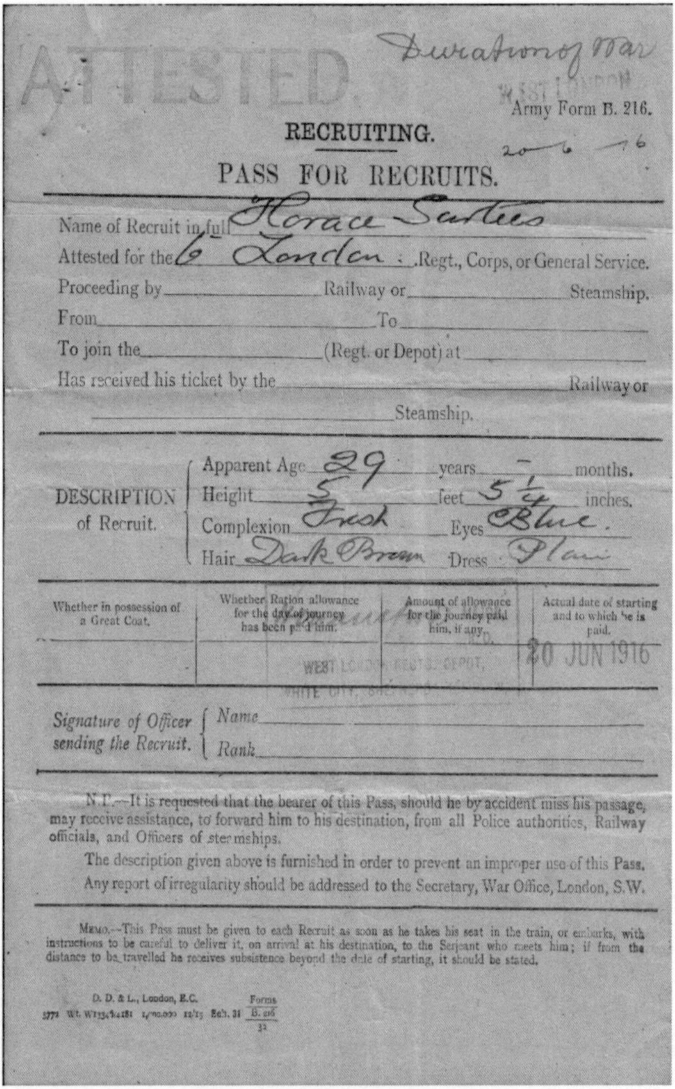
ATTESTED.

Duration of War

WEST LONDON

Army Form B. 216.

RECRUITING.

20 – 6 – 16

PASS FOR RECRUITS.

Name of Recruit in full Horace Surtees

Attested for the 6 London . Regt., Corps, or General Service.

Proceeding by ______ Railway or ______ Steamship.

From ______ To ______

To join the ______ (Regt. or Depot) at ______

Has received his ticket by the ______ Railway or ______ Steamship.

DESCRIPTION of Recruit.

Apparent Age 29 years – months.
Height 5 feet 5 1/4 inches.
Complexion Fresh Eyes Blue.
Hair Dark Brown Dress Plain

Whether in possession of a Great Coat.	Whether Ration allowance for the day of journey has been paid him.	Amount of allowance for the journey paid him, if any.	Actual date of starting and to which he is paid.
		WEST LONDON RECTG. DEPOT, WHITE CITY	20 JUN 1916

Signature of Officer sending the Recruit. *Name* ______ *Rank* ______

N.B.—It is requested that the bearer of this Pass, should he by accident miss his passage, may receive assistance, to forward him to his destination, from all Police authorities, Railway officials, and Officers of steamships.

The description given above is furnished in order to prevent an improper use of this Pass. Any report of irregularity should be addressed to the Secretary, War Office, London, S.W.

Memo.—This Pass must be given to each Recruit as soon as he takes his seat in the train, or embarks, with instructions to be careful to deliver it, on arrival at his destination, to the Serjeant who meets him; if from the distance to be travelled he receives subsistence beyond the date of starting, it should be stated.

D. D. & L., London, E.C.
5772 Wt. W1334/4181 1/100,000 12/15 Sch. 31 Forms B. 216 / 32

Plate 6. Enlistment paper.

Spend most of our money there. We get pay every Wednesday, five Francs. Just enough to last the week. Did I tell you we arrived on Sunday? We have an issue of two packets of Fags, B.D.V. One ounce of tobacco and a box of matches. Can always exchange tobacco for fags. The church parade here is nothing compared with ours in England. Well, my dear, think I told you all, so will now answer your letter. Let me know if you receive all my letters. As you will see I date all mine, simply say letter dated so and so and then I know if you don't get them. Will you be good enough to send me a paper now and again? Any paper will do. Get no news here. Glad to hear you took parting well, as we are far from one another. I am always thinking of you and little Maggie. No, I think 10/- was cheap taking it all around. We were lucky to get a place so quick. I don't think you can grumble. Anyhow, we can afford it. Put all your expenses down to my account. Dogs body had a letter from Mrs Reading, she has got photos all right. Don't send me any. The others are having theirs sent here, so I shall see one. Understood. George was at Liverpool. How did those photos turn out he took? Have you seen any?

No, have not had letter from Mother yet, if sent to Hurdcott will be forwarded on here, give them a few days longer. Will let you know later if I get it or not. Keep the counterfoil. Don't talk about food, enough to make a man cry. Don't send me any parcels while I'm here. I have enough money to buy food with, you need not send me any money, please. Yes, I know you are always prepared to do the best for me, there is nothing I want. Yes. I take great care of myself. You do the same. Will write to you often as possible. Enclosing you two postcards(Plates 11). One of our badges and one of Havre. Will send you some more later. Take great care of them. I consider they are good. Well, my dear, have told you all, so must dry up, hoping this will find you and little Maggie in the best of health and spirits. With very best love from your loving husband Horace. PS Posted on Sunday 15.

So, Horace is beginning to settle into his new life but finding some things strange. The foreign currency, the cost of simple necessities such as cigarettes and his favourite postcards. Also, the training he is undergoing to fit him for his task as a soldier. It hasn't yet sunk in that the skills of bombing and bayoneting are not just training exercises. His thoughts still rest a great deal with his family and he cares a great deal for their wellbeing. The lecture from the officer in which he emphasised the need to keep the people back home informed and assured of their loved ones' health and good spirits.

The next letter has been heavily censored over the first two pages and only the third and fourth pages were permitted to be sent home. The date has also been obliterated but is probably 14 or 15 October 1916.

"Hoping that little Maggie is processing well after her bite. Bet she didn't half cry. I could picture her face. Let me know how she is and thank her for long letter. Expect she was pleased when you enclosed it. Thanks for Daily Mirror received Friday. Yes, I think it is four cards, anyhow you have had all my letters so must be right. Enclosing you one tonight (Plate 12). Very good. Bought card for the ivy around the cross. Consider lovely card, not because I am religious. Anyhow one towards your collection. Have had no mails here for two days. Expect trouble in the channel. Sending card to Mother (Plate 13). The words are "To my dear mother". Would you like one of Dick Heaton's Regiment? Can get them here. If you don't hear from me much this week, don't be alarmed. On the Fatigue Party at the docks. Have no time to write or do anything. Some mornings, I don't have time to wash or do anything. Up at ¼ to 5. Have breakfast at 5:15, off to the docks, get back about 9 at night. Look around, have a wash. At 10, lights out. So, you can see that I haven't got time to write and the same the following days, but today they have given us a rest. Might tell you can do with it. Have been sleeping nearly all day. Well, my dear, have no more to tell you so must dry up, wishing you and little Maggie the best of luck, with very best love and kisses, from your loving husband, Horace.

Plate 7. The Ferry to France.

One can only wonder at what highly secret item of information came into Horace's possession that had to be expunged by the censor. Something he had seen or heard about during his work in the docks perhaps? It is obvious that he has been working very hard and falls into an exhausted sleep when he returns to his tent.

By Friday, 20 October, he is able to find time to resume his letter writing.

My dearest darling Maggie,

Thanks for letter tonight, dated Tuesday. Glad to hear you and little Maggie are first rate. Myself in the best of health. So sorry to hear you are having bad weather. Been rotten here. Left off raining last night but today's been nice but cold. Taking to wearing my cardigan. Mr Powell is here, you know who I mean, with some more. Most amusing, he wants to know what his wife will do. Told him, she will have to do the same as others. Wrote you three letters this week: Sunday, Wednesday, Thursday and one now. In the others, have enclosed some nice silk postcards (Plates 14 and 15). Hoping you have got them all right. Will now answer your kind letter.

Expect things are quiet at Southfields now all the boys are away. Yes, I know you sooner be in your own bed, I know I should. Am afraid I will forget what bed is the time I come out of this job. Don't you worry yourself about the war, keep your mind off of it and everything will be all right. Had letter from Mother telling me about George. All I can say is that he is a hero. Don't expect we shall meet out here because we are in different regiments. Glad you are pleased with the photo (Plate 10). Myself highly delighted with them. As you say, they are like life. Hoping you will look after one of them, don't send me one, have seen them. Send those along that George took. Don't matter how ugly they are, that your old cry, saying that you spoilt them. Every time you have yours taken, you turn around and say you spoilt them but that don't work. Kindly remember me to Mr Mrs Moore, also Hay. Tell them for me that I am all merry and bright under the circumstances. The Zepps won't hurt you, they don't like Fulham. Told you in my last letter what I want. Please don't send me any parcels yet. I will take great care of myself, leave all that to me. One thing I ask you to do is don't worry about me and things will be all right. Wrote to Con last night. He will have a blue fit. Take him all day to read it, five pages. First time that I ever written to him. Letter and photo from Arthur, very good of him. Moved to Evershot, Surrey. One from the old man, still very busy. Well, my dear, have no more to tell you so must dry up with very best love and kisses to you and little Maggie, from your loving husband, Horace. Cheer O dear, Goodnight, keep smiling.

Plate 8. To Maggie, from the camp at Le Havre.

Plate 9. To 'Little Maggie'. Note the Allied flags on the birds.

It would seem that Maggie is becoming concerned about Horace being so far away and facing war and Horace is doing his best to soothe her. The Zeppelins have been flying near to, and over London and dropping bombs. Horace's comment that they don't like Fulham may well have caused a wry smile at home. Arthur is his elder brother, who has apparently moved away from London. Some more silk postcards have been sent to add to the growing collection.

The next letter is dated Monday, 23 October 1916, same address.

My dearest darling Maggie,

Thanks for kind long letter received tonight, also paper dated Friday, 20 October. Glad to hear you and little Maggie are in the best of health and spirits, myself first rate all merry and bright. Will answer your letter further on.

The weather has changed, very cold in the morning, but lovely in the afternoon. For instance, today been lovely sunshine, just like a day in August. Saturday and Sunday mornings had white frost. Damme if I could keep warm in bed. Lovely washing under the cold water tap at five in the morning. Unable to write to you yesterday, collared me for guard last Saturday night. Starts from 7 am Sunday to Monday morning about 9, time we are dismissed. This being my first guard was not so bad. Had nice fire and plenty to eat. Forgot to take writing paper with me of course. Couldn't write. Sooner be on guard than stuck about the camp on Sunday, nothing to do, give one the pip. No fire or anything else. Had all our tent, 12 of us, so was with some of the lads and things went off all right. Am enclosing you another post card (Plate 16). No doubt you will say it very good. Anyhow I do. Will send you some more later on (If you behave yourself). Well, my dear, will now answer your kind letter. Very glad you like these postcards. Will make good keepsakes, will have them framed and give to Maggie, something for her to look at when grows older and to treasure. Sorry to hear you've been having bad weather. Don't talk about winds. You can guess how we feel the wind here in this open country. Think yourself lucky if you can stand up. Yes, as you say, one cannot help thinking of one another these terrible days. I, myself, am thinking of you both day and night. No dear, don't send me any parcels please. Thanking you for your kind offer. Have money, can buy what I want. Papers are very useful here. Cannot buy Sunday papers here. They are always welcome. Mr Best Birt is still going great. No, as you say, No GREYHOUND here. There is a beer canteen here but I haven't sampled any yet, so cannot say much about French beer. If I remain long in France without any will be TT when I come home. Don't talk about eggs. Have seen none yet. They say we can buy them at 3d each and cost about 4d to have them boiled. Will be very dear eggs, 2 for 10d. Have met no more fellows yet. Rather strange how one runs across another. He married and has a girl, tells me the baby is queer. May meet Gulliver, no telling who you do meet. Hope I do. I must say some of the Officers are very nice. Of course, they are mostly married and know what things are. Will write to Mrs Hay sometime this week. Glad you found them all well. Daresay she was surprised that I was taking a holiday in France. Don't worry about that letter, not worth the trouble. The post office will want to know your age, how many children you got, marriage lines and so forth and after six months will turn around and say sorry cannot trace postal order. Wear that amount of boot leather off making enquiries. No use unless you know date and so and so. Let it drop, hoping the person who stole letter and PO falls down and breaks his b--- neck. Hoop another good toy as long as it keeps her quiet that all right. Daresay she has seen some other little girl with one. I will take great care of myself; you do the same and things will be all right. There are two more letters to come, dated 19th and 20th. Well dear, cannot think of any more to say so must dry up, with very best love and kisses to you and little Maggie. Hoping these few lines will find you in the pink. Kindly remember me to Mr and Mrs Moore. From your loving husband, Horace.

Plate 10. 'The Four of Us'. Horace is rear row, right.

Plate 11. The flags of the allies.

Excuse writing, can hardly keep my eyes open, had no sleep for 40 hours so you can guess how I feel. Did not want to keep you too long without letter. Goodnight dear.

It would seem that Maggie has sent a postal order in one of her letters and that it has not arrived, probably stolen. With Horace's experience of the post office and its workings, he seems to think it's not worth the effort to try and recover it. One can only wonder at what it is that has kept him awake for forty hours. More labour at the docks or maybe military manoeuvres?

His next letter is dated Wednesday, 25 October.

My dearest darling Maggie,

Thanks for letter dated Friday 20th and parcel and etc posted Monday. Everything is all right. Just the things. Will answer them further on. Glad to hear you and little Maggie are in the best of health. Myself in the pink. Weather has changed again, raining Tuesday, left off at dinnertime, early this morning raining again, afternoon was grand. Had long day at docks yesterday, unloading and stacking timber makes a long day. Up at 4:45 in the morning, get back to camp at 9 pm. Anyhow, made a bit of a change. Today touched lucky, in camp getting ready and giving out things to a big draft arrived today. Some of our fellows amongst them. One fellow I knew from S.W. Letters, he spotted me. Had nice meals at Havre, went down by tram, not a bit like London trams. More ride on the driver's platform than inside. Had letter from May telling me that all are well at Southfields. Will now answer your kind letters, first dated Friday, 20 October. Glad you like cards so much. Sorry you have such bad weather, the same as us. Don't talk about fires. They are things of the past in the army. Yes, no doubt if you were here you do your very best for me. No dear, don't trouble to send me any parcels, thank you for your kind offer. Papers are very handy here, about the only thing we cannot get. No, any papers will suit me you like to send. Just discovered that I answered your letter dated 20th so will go no further. One posted Sunday. Glad little Maggie was pleased with PC. I can picture her face when she saw it. Have plenty of money, got about 15 francs now. Mr Taylor is a good sort. I know for a fact that he often makes enquiries concerning the men's club. Should pay Mr Eland 4d per week, perhaps the Club is a bit shaky owing to members being killed. Yes, I have received all your letters and answered them all. You forget it takes time, about five days by the time you post it and the time you get my letters in Fulham. If you look it up, you will find I have. Yes, the case and pocketbook is just the thing, just my handwriting. Awfully good of you to send photo of Maggie, why not send one of yourself to match it. Am laying on my belly in the tent writing this letter. Very comfortable condition. Well dear, have no more to tell you so must dry up with very best love and kisses to you and Maggie, from your loving husband, Horace.

Plate 12. Regimental badge of City of London Rifles.

Plate 13. He liked the ivy around the cross.

Once again Horace has been kept busy on fatigues, this time unloading timber at the docks. Another large draft of men has arrived to swell the growing armies. It must be quite cold, yet the soldiers are not allowed fires to keep them warm? At least, they are getting paid and no doubt there is plenty in the canteens and cafes to help separate the soldier and his pay. Back home there appears to be some problem with "the Club", probably a savings and loan club. The Surtees' family contribution would seem to be 4d per week. Obviously with the growing casualty lists many of the members are being lost and this is causing some loss of income to the club.

The next letter is dated Thursday, 26 October, from the same address.

My Dearest darling Maggie,

Thanks for kind letter received today, dated Monday, October 23. Glad to hear you and little Maggie are in the best of health. Myself in the pink. Had a nice storm in the middle of the night and a bit showering this morning so you can guess there's plenty of mud about. Fell in for a nice job today, helping to cart the waste away from the cookhouse and taking same to a farm. Some lovely smells from it, also make our clothes dirty and greasy. Plenty more where they come from. Had a glorious hot water bath today. Managed to wash my flannel shirt all right. Just had issue of belly belt. Just about fit, Mother! Letter from Tom tonight, still going great. Also written long letter to Mrs Hay tonight. Wrote you last night so have not much to tell you. Will now answer your letter. Sorry to hear about Maggie. Can guess how she cried. Cannot blame the Rabbit, accident. Don't suppose there will be much trouble about parting with it. Now the time to get rid of it. Not much good to us, only trouble to us. Let me know how she is progressing. Give it to who you like, less work for me when I come home. The weather in London is same as here, very changeable indeed. Don't send my scarf until I go up the line. Not cold enough for that yet. What a funny girl you are. Keep writing and telling you that I answer letter dated so and so. You keep count and see for yourself. Have got all your letters, also two Daily Mirrors also parcel. You forgot it takes three days before I have them and the same when I write. You want things done quick. Will you forward me soon as possible one of those photos (4 of us) as I want the others to sign it? Will return back. Don't trouble about Postman's Gazette, not much in them. Heard about raids. Well, my love, have told you all at present so must dry up, hoping this will find you in best of spirits also hoping little Maggie is getting on all right. With very best love and kisses, from your loving husband, Horace.

Plate 14. Postcard sent to Mrs Surtees, Senior.

Plate 15. And Mrs Surtees, Junior.

PS. Little Maggie, tell her to be careful next time. She will soon be better.

The joys of the simple things! A hot water bath and the chance to wash some clothes. It seems the business of selling kitchen waste to local farmers is a long established one in the army. As Horace says, it's a mucky job, particularly using the tools and equipment of his age. Little Maggie has suffered some accident with her pet rabbit. It bit her. So, it seems the rabbit must go. No doubt in a London undergoing a food rationing, there will be no difficulty in disposing of it. And news of the air raids has reached the troops in France. The next letter is to bring news of a surprise move.

Monday, 30 October, Private H. Surtees 400
1st Royal Inniskilling Fusiliers
B.E.F. France.
My Dearest darling Maggie,
Just a line letting you know that I am leaving this camp tonight, don't know where to. Also, that I have been transferred to an Irish Regt. By the above. Don't write to me until you hear from me. Rather disappointing changing us like that, but still will have to put up with it. Letters you have written will be forwarded. Glad to say cold is much better today. Having terrible weather here today, stormy all day, up to our eyes in mud. Have no more to say, wrote you last night so must dry up with very best love and kisses to you and little Maggie. Hoping both are in the best of health, from your loving husband, Horace.
X for little Maggie, hope her finger is better.

Plate 16. A Christmas card purchased locally. (Y.M.C.A. Shop?)

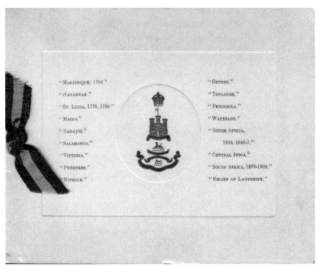

Plate 17. Regimental Christmas Card. Originally sold in the Dardenelles. Given away in France (in the new year).

So, Horace is on the move, probably up the line and with a new regiment. Where he is going and how he will get on with his new comrades will no doubt be revealed when he gets down to resuming his letter writing again. Which he does on Sunday, 5 November 1916.

Private H Surtees 40055
C Coy 12 Platoon
1st Royal Inniskilling Fusiliers
B.E.F.
My Dearest darling Maggie,

Just a line letting you know that I am in the best of health and spirits. Having some good weather for time of year. No doubt by now that you know I am transferred to an Irish Regt. Not only our regt but several more regts. Was quite a surprise on Monday. Just that we were going to be transferred. Of course, we had no say in the matter. I believe it's the usual thing now to transfer men from one regt to another. Left Harvre (sic) Monday night and after two days, railway journey reached our regt. Had Tuesday morning in Rouen, sent you some postcards (Plate 17). Could not see much of Rouen. Was in rest camp. What bit I did see was pretty. We were down by the river Seine. Much better than our river Thames, the portion we were at. We reach our regt on Wednesday night. As usual raining. Our camp was on once a battlefield, cannot mention name. Was awful muddy, worst place ever been in. Jolly glad to leave it. They gave us a parting shell. Friday was moved further down in billets. Am in some farm sheds. Some in stables, some up in loft. Myself up in the loft, the four of us. Fairly large village puts me in mind of Bicester. We are allowed in the village. If we want to go further, we have to get a pass. Having one today. We were lucky our regt is resting. Had concert here last night. Some Irish songs, also English. Passed a few minutes away. Some very nice tea here, best I tasted since I left England. Sample some of the French beer here. Much better than Harvre. You can picture us four sitting in café amongst French people. One of us can speak French so we are all right. Also speak German and Spanish. The fellow in photo of four, the stoutest one. Nearly all English (sounds rather funny, Englishmen in an

Irish regt) Some of these Irishmen want some understanding. This address will find me anywhere so when writing, put this address. Never thought I should be in the regular army but anyhow I am. Daresay your separation papers will be all right, that won't be much trouble to either side. Don't worry about me. Had no letters since last Friday week. Have written letters to you dated 23, 25, 26, 29 and 30 October and 4 postcards dated 31 October.

The Harbour was closed for four days, so expect will have them together. How is little Maggie? Most anxious to know. Daresay her finger is all right by now, anyhow, hope so.

Unfortunately, the letter ends there. The rest of it somehow did not survive the years since 1916. Horace seems fatalistic, as usual, about his transfer to the Irish Regiment. It would seem that the Inniskillings had suffered severe casualties and needed to make up their numbers, so the base camp at Le Havre was called upon to find replacements. The Royal Inniskilling Fusiliers had taken part in the battle of the Somme, which commenced on 1 July 1916 and was still in its final stages at this time. (November 1916). Horace's draft of replacements had a long train journey from Le Havre to Rouen, which is not a great distance, some 60 kilometres in a straight line. Due no doubt to the chaotic state of the railway system and the disruptions caused by the battle this short distance took two days to cover by train. It is not clear which camp was shelled but it would be more likely to be the reception camp at Rouen rather than Le Havre. Wherever it was, Horace and his comrades were quickly moved on to the farm buildings in the village. The troops are now allowed a greater degree of freedom to get out than they did at the base camp. A stroll into the village, or further if they get a pass. He and his three close friends (the four of us) have been into the village and tried out the delights of a café and French beer! Luckily for them, one of their numbers speaks French. The next letter is dated Thursday, 9 November 1916.

Dearest darling Maggie,

Just a line letting you know that I am still alive and kicking. In the best of health and spirits hoping you and little Maggie are the same. The weather here is rotten, nothing but rain. Wake up in the morning, it's raining. The same at bedtime. Gives one the fair pip. Wouldn't mind so much if we had somewhere to dry our clothes. Had no letters from you for a fortnight. Expect they are hung up somewhere in the port. Received letter from Southfields yesterday dated 29 October, forwarded from Harvre. They sent me a parcel on Monday, 30 October. Have not got it yet. Daresay it will be in fine condition when I do. Don't send me my scarf. Have been issued with one today. Hand made by the look of it. You can picture me sleeping in the loft, also climbing up and down the ladder. Some job! This loft is all right for a man suffering from consumption who requires open air treatment. Got quite used to it now. You ought to see me in my steel helmet, you would have a fit. Also my leather jacket, fleecy lined, nice and warm. Regt still resting, have plenty of parades. In fact, it's all parades. As soon as we sit down someone shouts, "Fall in."

Some inspection on. You know what faces I used to pull when drinking rum or rather one or two mouthfuls. Lost all that now. Had an issue of rum this week. Not bad stuff. Sample some French Red wine. Just like drinking vinegar. No more of that for me. Like their liquors but cost too much. The boys here told me that I was shouting out "Maggie", in my sleep last night, so expect I was thinking of you. Don't remember saying anything. How is little Maggie getting on? Hope her finger is all right by now. Have you got rid of that rabbit yet? Well, my dear, have no more to say so must close with very best love and kisses to you and little Maggie, from your loving husband, Horace.

The new arrivals have now begun to get their fighting equipment. Steel helmets, fleece lined leather jackets and no doubt all the rest of the paraphernalia, which the soldier of 1916 was required to carry. Conditions are not of the best, although no doubt the veterans of the Somme considered themselves in relative comfort and safety. The issuing of Rum was very much a part of front-line rations and Horace can definitely consider himself to be on active service. The commanders were all of the opinion that idle men became disgruntled men and so did their best to fill the waking hours. Parades, inspections, route marches, were all used to ensure that the troops did not have enough time to sit around and think about their conditions or why they were there. In the few moments relaxation that was allowed Horace and his friends have obviously been down to the village again, this time to sample the delights of French wine. The ubiquitous Vin Rouge, which almost every soldier of the Great War remembers with varying degrees of affection or dislike. Still concerned about little Maggie and her injury Horace has had no mail from his wife to offer him any comfort. He writes again to Maggie on Sunday, 12 November.

My dearest darling Maggie,

Just a line letting you know I am still in the best of health and spirits hoping you and little Maggie are the same. Having some nice weather now, no rain for two days (O what a change). Still resting in our lovely billet. What with my steel helmet, leather coat, vest, scarf, gloves and etc., will require a horse and cart to carry them. Received two papers yesterday forwarded from Harvre. The first for a fortnight. Lloyds and Sunday Pictorial. First paper I have seen for a long time. Had letter from Southfields last Wednesday and a letter and parcel yesterday. Glad to hear they are keeping well, like myself. All forwarded from Harvre. Lucky only one apple was bad, biscuits were broken. Not bad, no doubt had plenty of knocking about. Contained two apples, sardines, biscuits, sweets, walnuts, candles, cake, butter. You can guess us four had a good tea yesterday. We get butter here about three times every week, and very good butter too. Was in a village last night, cannot mention name, trying to buy young Maggie a present but unable to get anything. Will buy her something one of these days. Prices of stuff is very high here. For instance, Woodbines 2d a packet, Players 10's are 6d. So, you can see that things are double the price. Sorry to hear you are having such rotten weather, all rain. That's all we have seen lately.

Wake up in the morning raining, go to bed raining. So, you can see we have plenty of it. Yes, I know what it is to write when she's about. I also hope that this war will soon be over. Looking after myself all right. Hoping you are doing the same. Tell little Maggie I will soon be home again. Well my dear, have no more to say now so must close, with very best love and kisses to you and little Maggie, from your loving husband, Horace. PS Hoping to hear from you soon. No letter since last Wednesday fortnight. Cheer O dear. Sending you PC also one for Maggie.

So, another two weeks since Horace heard from his wife and daughter. No doubt he read in the paper that it had been raining hard at home. The receipt of a food parcel has done a lot to raise his spirits. Typically, it is shared with his three close friends. Prices of simple necessities like cigarettes strike him as very high. Double what he is used to in England. That means that a packet of Woodbines was normally 1d. That would be for a packet of five cigarettes. He is still keeping up the flow of postcards home and is obviously anxious to hear from his family. His next letter home is much happier, after finally receiving his long-awaited mail.

Friday, 24 November
My Dearest darling Maggie,
Just a line letting you know that I'm still alive and kicking, in the best of health and spirits. Glad to hear you are feeling better now. Have received all your letters and four lots of papers, also parcel. Will answer them in their turn. Having some nice weather but very cold at night. Cannot grumble for time of year. Sorry to keep you long time without letters. Had no letters collected for about 12 days, so you can see it isn't my fault. If I don't write often, don't you worry. We have been on the move from one place to another. Left our billets last Tuesday week. Been to three camps. Just come back from the trenches for another rest. Was very cold up in the trenches, frosty nights. Had eight letters from Harve, one from Con, one

36

from Taylor, two from you, one Father, one Arthur, one Hampshire, one Tom, so you can see I shall be busy answering them. Letter dated Monday, 30 October. Glad to hear Maggie's finger is all right. Now expect she fed up with the rabbit. Good job too. Daresay straw and food are very dear now. No fear of you breaking the man's camera. Think it over. That photo of us I think is very good indeed. Highly pleased with it. No, my rise is due on 25 May. Used to be 25 August. If they are paying you too much they soon wake up and find out their mistake. I can pretty well guess prices of food and etc is very dear. Long time before they will be cheaper. Anyhow, do your best and don't strain yourself. We get pay now and again, only when we are in billets. Other times, cannot spend it. Had letter from Father telling me about stopping of money. Will write to pay girl Heaton when I have time. My flannel shirts are all right. I can mend them myself. Tell little Maggie I shall have to learn shorthand to read her letter.

Friday morning, 3 November

About that letter you expect, spoke to them straight. They didn't like it, will tell you all about it when I come home. As you say, when one in the Army, that good enough. No, your letters are not touched, you can say what you like. Will try and get PC for you if there's a chance to get them.

Tuesday, 14 November.

Daresay the cause of your sickness was catching cold and worry yourself about the war. If I was you, don't worry. I am fit and well. Not worrying, so you do the same, will be like me, all merry and bright. Now buck yourself up. Never mind about the war, that will soon be over. Now, about photo. I borrow one from Mr Harradine, thinking perhaps the one you sent was lost. So, he can have yours, the one you sent. Make no difference. You will find it signed.

Yes, give the rabbit to Con, or anyone who wants it. Daresay you will be glad to see the back of it for goodness sake. Yes, getting used to drinking Rum. Don't mind it at all. Had four spoonfuls of it in the trenches. Rare stuff to warm us up. Had bottles of white and red wine. Can buy them for 1/8

d. Don't care much for red wine. Never tried it hot. We are allowed in certain cafes. No, cannot buy whisky out here. Had letter from Tom telling me about meeting Walter and Arthur. What I see, he is meeting everyone.

Sunday, 19 November

We have good food when we can get it, so don't trouble to send many parcels. One now and again. Don't send biscuits, they were in crumbs. Send me some homemade small cakes. Yes, will do my utmost best to try and get little Maggie a present of some kind before I come home. No, we get plenty of fags. Can buy them in YMCA cheap. In fact, cheaper there than in England because there's no tax on them. About those two PCs, They were handed back to me. Was not allowed to send them because they have the name of village on them. I have them still in my pocket.

Tuesday, 7 November

We were only at Rouen a few hours, so Jack Gulliver must be further up. He only landed there in a camp the same as I was at Havre. He was behind the firing line somewhere. I always destroy your letters when I answer them, less to carry about. I was surprised to hear from Southfield that you allow little Maggie to leave you for one night, what happened to you? If I was you, I would chalk it up. Have not got fags from Mr Taylor. Expect they are on the road here. Yes, have still got ring. At present time, is lovely and muddy.

Thursday, 9 November

No, will not forget (S) when the time comes. Tom landed at Rouen so we have all been there. You will see which is Harradine, our Frenchman, when you get this letter.

Monday morning. Thank you very much for parcel. Everything all right barring biscuits, they were all crumbs. Was a welcome parcel. Come from the trenches and found that waiting for me. What a feed we had Hankies are just the thing; others are beginning to wear out. Papers are just the right thing, come in handy in many ways.

Well dear, don't send me many papers. Don't get much time for reading. Had to leave a lot at the billet. I think if you send me one book of Daily Mirrors about every three weeks will do. If you send too many, they are only destroyed and the money wasted. Well, my dear, think I have answered all your letters. Had so many. Just received Daily Mirror and Lloyds Postman's Gazette. I think I had about six lots of papers. Anyhow, daresay have got all you sent. They give us some Oxo cubes now and again so don't trouble to send any. Have scarf gloves and mittens. Thank little Maggie for chocolate. Just right. Eat more chocolate in France than in England. Always buying it. Buy it one franc at a time. Spent nearly all my money on chocolate. Give her a big kiss from me. Tell her I shall not forget her. Well dear, have told you all so must close. Wishing you the best of health with very best love and kisses to you and little Maggie. From your loving husband, Horace.

Well, what a lot of letters must have been waiting for Horace when he came out of the line. And how he must have leapt upon them and read and re-read them. Having read them, he then set out to reply to each point Maggie had made in her letters, taking each in turn. He has obviously spent a long period in the trenches, and comments on the cold. He chides Maggie gently for worrying too much and tells her to be like him, all merry and bright. The fate of the rabbit that bit little Maggie is still in the balance, he suggests giving it to brother Con, or anyone that wants it! He is enjoying the Rum ration, issued to the soldiers whilst in the trenches to try to keep them a little warmer but isn't very keen on wine, red or white. The mention of 'trying it hot' is intriguing. He is slowly changing his ideas about food parcels. When at Le Havre he was adamant that Maggie was not to send any. Now, he is beginning to look forward to some comforts from home and asking for some little homemade cakes. Chocolate now forms the main part of his purchases and he is eating more than he did in England. Being a source of energy, he can be forgiven for taking all he can get.

1916 is slowly coming to its end and to open the last month of that year, Horace writes to Maggie again on Friday, 1 December 1916.

My dearest darling Maggie,

Just a line letting you know I am in the best of health and spirits. Hoping you and little Maggie are the same. Thank you very much for Daily Mirror posted Thursday, 23 November. Glad to hear you are going great. Having some dry weather now but very cold and frosty at nights. Don't mind the cold as long as it keeps dry. Daresay the weather in London is just the same. Looks very pretty in the mornings to see the frost hanging everywhere but dammed cold. Sorry not written before. Been up again and back tonight to huts for little rest. Been no letters collected since last Sunday. Hope you have received my letter written last Friday, also photo inside letter. Just heard you have written to Miss Reading making inquiries. But dear, don't worry if I don't write for some days. Will write to you as soon and as often as I can. Sometimes we cannot send letters but we can always get letters sent to us.

Forgot to tell you in my last letter, you asked about green envelopes. Yes, have stopped them. Those envelopes you sent me have stuck together, and of course are no use. I think when you write to me, put me in about two envelopes, that will do. The heat from body soon does them in. Just the same if I put them in pack. About the Daily Mirror. Just been thinking it over. If you send me two now and again will do. Have not read the three you sent. Had to throw away two. Nowhere to put them and a bit heavy to carry about on these roads. Enough to do to carry myself about on these roads. Just had three days in a dugout. Not so bad, put me in mind of going down a mine. Last Sunday we had an issue of Xmas Pudding, a nice piece. It was great, made by Harrods Stores. It was good, thought it was Xmas Day. Last Monday, had a nice hot water shower bath. Took us about eight hours to go there and back, also had clean change. Had to throw flannel shirt away. If I didn't it might have walked away. Got a good warm undershirt, felt different altogether after that bath, it was grand. According to what I can hear, London looks somewhat rotten now. The shops close much earlier. Looks like being a rotten Xmas for some of them. Don't suppose I shall have to work so hard this Xmas as I have done in years past. Be a bit of a change for me. About that 13/- you got. Been reading the Postman's Gazette. Have given us 1/- more War bonus. 1/- for males, 6d for females, so you are all right. Might have made it10/-. Been more like it. Anyhow, a little is better than none at all. Have not received those fags from Mr Taylor. When you see him, tell him will answer his letter dated 24 October when I have time. Received it on 16 November. Hope you have a decent share out from him. Tell him all merry and bright under the circumstances. Well my dear, have not a lot of news for you this time, so must dry up with very best love and kisses to you and little Maggie. Kindly remember me to Mr and Mrs Moore and all, from your loving husband, Horace.

X for little Maggie. Tell her will soon be home again, hoping she is keeping a good girl. Goodnight dear. Just going to bed, feel somewhat sleepy.

So, it is still cold and damp in the trenches, but 'looks very pretty in the mornings'. Horace says that he has spent some time in a dugout. Maybe he has been doing some special job that has kept him under the shelter rather than out in the open trenches Christmas has come a little early for him and his comrades, with an issue of Harrods's Christmas pudding. But more than that, he has had a hot bath! What a joy that must have been, followed by a complete change of clothing, even down to his beloved flannel shirt which has been his constant companion since arriving in France. As he said, it almost walked away! He is thinking back to the Christmases past, which are the busiest time of year for the postmen and commenting that he won't have to work so hard this year. The Post Office is continuing to pay Maggie a small sum to make up his army pay and this it seems, has been increased by 1/- per week. Which draws the comment that 10/- would be more appropriate. Mr Taylor apparently runs a savings and loan club and the annual share-out is due. We hope that Maggie received a good return on her investment.

The next letter is dated 14 December 1916.
My dearest darling Maggie,

Just a line letting you know I am in the best of health and spirits. Glad to hear you and little Maggie are the same. Have received your letter dated 28 November and 5 December, also Postman Gazette and Lloyds dated 26 November, daily Mirror had on Tuesday. Will answer them later on in letter. Been no letters collected since last Sunday week, so you can see why I have not written before. As you know I will write when there is a chance. Having some changeable weather now. Was dry and cold up to last Friday, but since then been raining and there is some mud about now. Things are all very busy in London now. If I were there now, I would be doing some extra for money. Now I do it for nothing. I think it works out about a farthing an hour (Oh, what a game). Never mind, will be home for the next. Had parcel from May last Monday, was 'Tray bon' (a bit of French!) small cakes, short bread, nuts, sweets, chocolate. Came just the right time. We were looking in shop windows but afraid to spend our money. We had glorious supper that night. Sent you a card last Monday (Plate 20). Hope you will like it. Cost one franc. Very dear here. In fact, everything very high. Halfpenny cakes in London cost two and halfpence. With our little money, we have to be careful. Time, we brought some bread don't go far. Did you get that photo? You never mention so in your letter. The one of four of us. Have received your letter dated Sunday, 10 December, also paper Lloyds.

Letter from Tom. Hurt his knee playing football. Got water on the knee. Will always suffer from that. Only wants a slight knock, up it will come again. He is still going great. He is going to find out where our division is. I am in the 29th division, 87th Brigade. Should like to see him. Sorry to say I have just committed a crime, dropped out on a route march and got six days defaulters. Rotten job that can't have five minutes to ourselves. Anyhow, got over it all right. This place is fairly large. Can buy almost anything we want. Plenty of life. Seen none for some time. Ought to see us eating fried chips in paper for supper. Helps to fill hole up. Next pay day going to have fried egg and chips, bread and coffee for 1 Fr 25. Coffee very cheap here. Can get large basin for 2 ½.

Cannot get tea here. Only in first-class cafes. Will now answer your letter dated 10 December. Glad to hear you and little Maggie are keeping well. Also hope she is a good girl. By your letter, you are having the same kind of weather as us. About the Daily Mirror. Those big books. Have not a lot of time for reading. If you send me one now and again will do. I don't mean book. Had another bath yesterday and change of clothing. Yes, been alive-oh several times. Spend some time with a candle chasing them. Can always get plenty of socks. Glad you keep respectful hours like myself. I go to bed about 7 pm. We sleep when we can. Don't get much sleep in the trenches. Don't talk about money; you can do whatever you like with any money. The money is as much yours as mine, so I don't care what you do with it or where it goes. Enjoy yourself, but whatever you do, don't strain yourselves. Have plenty to eat or else you will have a breakdown, but don't do that please. So, Rose has a little girl. What a family the Youngs are, nothing but girls. But never mind that as long as they are all right. So, she will be full of troubles and hard up. Good job May don't care for it. Daresay she is enough trouble without somebody else's. No wonder Hampshire was married. These things leak out after a little time. Well dear have told you all at present so must dry up. Hoping you will have a happy Xmas, with fondest love and kisses to you and little Maggie, from your loving husband, Horace.

Life in the trenches is still wet and muddy and Horace is thinking of all the overtime he would be getting if he were still a postman, and comparing his wage then to his soldier's pay. Showing off his knowledge of French, too. Prices of foodstuffs are very high and he says they are afraid to spend their little bit of pay. However, he and his three close friends had a jolly good feast on the parcel, which his sister May had sent.

Share and share alike was the watchword for the soldiers at the front. Interesting comparison, halfpenny cakes in London are five times dearer in France. Horace has also fallen foul of Military discipline and suffered six days Defaulters for falling out whilst on a Route March. This off course took place whilst the troops were 'resting' behind the line. He mentions being able to buy a 'large basin of coffee' for 2½. Pence or francs? The large basin would be the traditional Normandy Coupe used to drink from. It is more like a basin to English eyes. Later, he talks of spending time with a candle chasing lice from his clothing. The soldiers soon found this to be the best way to rid some of these pests from their clothes but the occasional bath and issue of fresh clothes must have been a heaven-sent relief. Rose, mentioned on the last page, was Maggie's sister, who may have found it necessary to marry rather hurriedly. Horace is becoming more aware of the approaching seasonal festivities and wishes his wife and daughter a happy Xmas. It was a week later that he was able to write again.

Wednesday, 20 December
My dearest darling Maggie,
Just a line letting you know I am still about. Have somewhat rotten cold. Cannot shake it off. Also cough. In fact, everybody the same here. Bedtime cannot sleep for them coughing. We are in some barn with plenty of air holes all around. Cold at nights. Cannot sleep. We are beside a railway. Plenty of passing traffic. So, you can see we are all right. Be all right when the war is over. Having some cold weather now. Yesterday snow, today lovely sunshine but somewhat frosty. Don't mind the cold if it only keeps dry. Daresay you are having the same weather in London Came back from the trenches last Friday. Was jolly cold up there and raining hard on Friday. Been moving from one place to another since last Saturday and now we are landed now for about four weeks. That's as far as I can hear. We hear so many rumours. We are resting in a French Town. Plenty of shops of all kinds, much better place than the last. Best we had. Anyhow, we are out for Xmas, which will be very nice. You will not have to wait for me this Xmas. Expect we will have some kind of dinner. Some of our fellows are receiving Xmas parcels. Wonder if I shall be lucky. Eggleton had one the night we came back from the trenches. Contain a lovely cake. We soon put paid to that.

Just came the right time. The old chap wrote to me asking if he could send me anything. Wrote back and told him he can send me anything eatable. He is still very busy, same old thing, still going great. Had letter from Arthur, he is still going well. Tell me he has struck a rotten camp. Dead and alive hole, worse thing he complains of is, the beer is rotten. Alice is getting very thin, she worries herself a lot. Not much good doing that these days. He thinks she will have a nervous breakdown. He will shortly be home for six days. They were somewhat anxious about me at home. Had letter saying they were greatly relieved when they had letter from me. Can quite understand it but cannot help it. Always write to them the same time as you. Wrote to Mr Taylor, also to Tom and May, wishing them many happy returns of their birthday. I cannot find out yet where his company is. Nobody knows them, so we shall not meet each other. Believe he is the other side of France. Have got George's address. 8th Irish King's Liverpool Regt. Not with us. He is keeping well, also have plenty to do. No doubt he has, he's a busy bee. Line from Hampshire, he is still keeping well. Do you see her much now? Daresay she about the same, walking about with a long face, as though she as all the troubles in the world on her shoulders. Do you see much of Mrs Horrocks? Expect she's doing well now. Expect he's been home on leave by this time. The boys here are always singing that song we heard at the Gaiety (they wouldn't believe me). Nearly 12 months ago since we were there, believe on 18 December. We have plenty of singing here night-time. Soon get dark about 4:30, make such a long night. Generally, go to bed about 6 pm. Have a sleep while we can. Will now answer your letter dated 26 November. Have told you the reason why you never had letter from me. You are greatly relieved now. Letter dated 28 November. Had letter from home telling me that Mother was queer. What with us being away and worrying herself and getting old, soon pulls her down. Yes, will get Maggie a handkerchief. Can buy them here for 3 ½ francs. No doubt Con will wake up and come for the rabbit 12 months to come for it. If he doesn't come, give it to anyone who wants it. Letter dated 5

December. Heard you were worrying yourself about me. Can quite understand it. If we cannot send letters, same applies to PC. Yes, we arrange with one another in case one of us gets blown over. So that's all right. We been very lucky up to now. You ask me if I have been in action. Well, I have been under some shellfire. Came out all right. Yes, I would like a photo of you and Maggie. Going to have mine taken if there is a chance in this town. Fancy dropping bombs in Brompton Rd. Good job they didn't hit Harrods. No, you can put any news in your letter, they are not opened. Don't send me P.O. Terrible job to change. You can send me a shilling when you send a parcel. Present time have only 1d in my pocket. Hoping to be paid tomorrow. The reason I asked you to send cakes, they are articles we cannot get. The Hankies come in very handy. Using them now. (Ed. Next line torn off, probably by censor.) Sorry to hear about May, that due to changeable weather. She easily catches cold Hoping by now she herself again. Had letter from Arthur telling me about going to Emma. He at Lydd Gunnery School, where they passed their test. You can do whatever you like with our money. I don't care. Leave it all to you. Glad to hear you were honest when buying boots. I beat you, just had a pair given to me. Well dear, think I have told you all so must close with very best love and kisses to you and little Maggie. Hoping these lines will find you in the pink, from your loving husband, Horace.

Another chatty letter, with many indications as to what a soldier's life was like. He has a cold (not surprising having to sleep out in a trench in winter) and the billet he is in when out of the line is an old barn with lots of holes in it. To add to his misery the billet is beside a railway with lots of trains passing. Yet, he remains cheerful and concerned about the two Maggie's back home. He would appear to be set for a few weeks rest but rumours abound. A rather forlorn comment, "Some of the fellows are receiving xmas parcels, wonder if I shall be lucky." His friend Eggleton has had one, which was duly shared out between the four comrades. Lots a family chat about his brothers, who are also in the army, and the twins, May and Tom. A memory of pleasures shared when he and

Maggie visited the Gaiety and remembered the song, they didn't believe me. Maggie is naturally concerned when mail doesn't arrive and continues to query him about it. A present for little Maggie is possibly about to be sent, a handkerchief, of which many pretty variations were to be found, in embroidered lace. He has finally confessed to Maggie that he has seen some action, and been under shellfire. And he and his comrades have some arrangement going in case one of them gets "blown over". The torn off portion appeared at the bottom two or three lines of page 6. No indication, of course, as to what it referred. Now Christmas Day approaches, what will it bring for Horace Surtees, Rifleman.

Thursday, 26 December 1916.

My Dearest darling Maggie,

Thanks for letter dated Sunday, 17 December, also card from little Maggie. Glad to hear both are keeping well. Myself all right except cold. Cannot shake it off. I'll be all right someday. Weather somewhat changeable. Sunday was nice day, yesterday dull and gale blowing. Just like March winds. Away in some very quiet village. Cannot buy anything. Beer somewhat rotten. One glass enough for me. Left our regiment last Saturday to do some firing for about a week. In some empty house, soon made it comfortable. Very quiet Xmas for us. Firing up to 4 o' clock Sunday, and up to 12 o' clock Xmas day. Gave us the day off today for a change. Had the usual dinner for Xmas. No pudding. Had nice parcel from Mother last Wednesday. Pudding, pie, sardines, two kind of sausages, bacon, rolls, mince pies, also fags from Em. Save them all for Xmas day. Good job I did otherwise would have been very poor for us.

Wouldn't have known it was Xmas day. Pudding and pie were grand. Had nice letter and card from Mother. Very touching words in letter, very true words on card. Am sending them to you. Want them kept and looked after. First time Mother has written to me for a number of years. Been trying to buy you New Year card but failed. Will try again when I go back to Regt. Tell little Maggie very kind of her to send me a card. Will give her a big kiss when I come home. They tell me I shall not know her, because she has grown so. Wrote and thanked Mother for parcel, also each of the girls. Wrote them few lines separately. Daresay you will see them before you leave Southfields. Hope you enjoyed yourself this Xmas. Under the circumstances, expect it was very quiet without the boys there I was thinking of you all about dinnertime, sitting around the table. I am sitting on the ground and that's all. I was happy enough, knew very well you and all was all right. Hoping to be home by next Xmas, and back to civil life once again. Got Maggie a nice card, hoping she will like it. Had a nice supper one day last week. 2 fried eggs, chips and bread, 1 Fr 25. First egg I tasted since I landed in France. Was tray bon. Well dear, will now answer your welcome letter. You are always anxiously waiting for a letter. You will always have one, when there's a chance to write one. No use me writing every day, wouldn't have nothing to speak about, so you must have patience. I am always thinking of you both. Yes, Harradine and Lane are Machine Gunners, but they are still attached to our platoon. Only thing is that they are at different parts of the trench. We are together when we come out of the line. No, they have not parted us yet. Still hanging together and sharing our goods together. Like s--- to a blanket. Sorry to hear you are having rotten foggy weather in London. Bad time of year for that weather. Have seen no fog here yet, only mist in the early morning. I should think that enough for her. She cannot expect much from you this year. Can guess what a list of toys etc., she wants. Hoping she done well by hanging up her stocking. Hung mine up last Sunday but no luck. Card is very good, shall look after that. Heard a lot of German Peace terms for weeks past. Hoping they will come to some kind of terms and soon finish up. Read about changes in Cabinet might stir things up a bit? Had letter from Mr Glasson a little while ago. Will answer it when I have time. Cannot understand about post office money. Mistake somewhere. Have it cleared up. Go up to the office and ask for wages branch and you will see a man with gold braid around his hat, he will put you right. They will explain in full to you. Don't want to get in their debt, will never get out of it. Don't be afraid to go up. They like to see the men's wives sometimes. Just to hear how they are going on. Don't worry about your ring paper. They will send it to you when they are ready to alter the name. Our Depot is Londonderry, Ireland. Have not received your parcel yet, daresay will be waiting for me when I return to our Regt. You can guess I will enjoy it when I catch hold of it. I will do it a bit of good. The mince pies Mother sent arrived in crumbs, hope yours don't. Talking about chicken and ham, there are plenty of chickens where we are but we are not lucky enough to get one. No, I am not cross about you spending money. You can do what you like. The money is as much yours as mine but don't strain yourself. Have plenty to eat or else down you will go.

Don't want to hear that. Do whatever you like with money. Carry on with the clubs as usual. Was Mother satisfied with her share out? Is she carrying on? Wrote to Mr Taylor telling him I wish to carry on. Yes, certainly will excuse writing. Can understand all. Sorry to hear about your Chilblains. Rotten things to have. Hope you will understand this letter writing. This is somewhat awkward condition. As you know we have no tables. Writing this on my knee so you can guess how awkward it is. Don't know when I shall be able to post this letter. Writing on the off chance of getting it posted. If long time receiving it, you will know unable to post until I re-join my Regt. Well my dear, have told you all at present so must close wishing you and Maggie Happy New Year and the best of luck, with very best love and kisses, from your loving husband, Horace.

Not a very happy Christmas day then, for Horace and his comrades. Thank goodness he received a food parcel from Mother. One can imagine how he and the other three of his pals enjoyed that. I cannot but feel that the army could have made some token recognition of the day. After all, the regiment was resting out of the line. He talks fondly of 'little Maggie', and how she will have grown out of all recognition when he comes home. He has also been enjoying the delights of fried eggs and chips, the first since arriving in France. For someone brought up in the England of the early 1900s that must have been quite a deprivation. However, he has at least got the solace of regular letters from Maggie, and other members of his family. Rumours of an end to the war are apparently rife. Fuelled no doubt by the longing on both sides for the carnage to come to an end. As we now know, that was not to happen for another two years. It is not until 31 December 1916 that Horace is able to sit down and write another letter to Maggie.

Sunday, 31 December 1916

My dearest darling Maggie,

Just a line letting you know that I am still in the best of health and spirits. Have got rid of cold now. Very funny weather now. Had some nice rain last night but taking it all around cannot grumble for time of year. Just fancy, will soon be in another year. Hoping will be better than this for all of us. Just returned from church parade. First church service I've been to since I joined the 1st Inniskilling Fus. So, you can guess was a chance to sing some hymns. Came back last Sunday night and by all accounts those left behind done well. Hope you received Xmas card, green envelope, and one written last week. Written to Hampshire and Mrs Glasson today, will write to Mrs Heaton next time I do some writing. Will now answer your registered letter 18 December. What a funny girl you are, always anxiously waiting to hear from me. As you know, will always write when there is a chance. On the other hand, can guess how pleased you are when you receive letter from me. Yes, I am glad to get out of trenches for a while. Been lucky for parcels. One from you, Mother and May.

Just had that tin of chicken and ham and Xmas pudding, nuts, chocolate. Eggleton and Lane. Went down all right. Had a good feed. We are also going to have a high tea shortly. Yes, was thinking of you both when eating contents of parcel. Daresay Maggie done a lot towards making goods, if only with her tongue, could picture her standing on a chair handing stuff to you. Would like to see her if only for a short time. I guess she'll go mad. Thank her very much for chocolate. Also give her big kiss for me. X. Have not heard from Mr Taylor yet or received those fags he sent. Give him my regards when you see him again. Well Maggie, have not a lot of news this time for you, so must close, wishing you both a Happy New Year and the best of luck for coming year, with very best love and kisses to you and little Maggie, from your loving Husband, Horace. Cheer O, dear. X for little Maggie, tell her I am still fighting Germans.

Have just written a few lines to Mrs Heaton tonight. Think we are leaving this billet at the end of this week for another.

Have lost my pocketknife, the one Tom and May gave me on my 21st birthday. They have given us a day rest today, so give me time to answer a few letters, goodbye dear, Horace.

Have received your letter 5 January, parcel and two Mirror, Saturday 13. Letter following this letter was written last Wednesday but owing to being on the move not collected.

And so Horace moves on into 1917. At least he and his friends had another good feast from the food parcels sent by his loving family. As is to be expected, his thoughts are with his wife and the child he has not seen for a long time. Little Maggie is missing her daddy and has been helping Mum to pack up a parcel for him. One can imagine her excitement and longing to see him again. The Regiment are moving about a lot and the sending and receiving of mail has obviously suffered due to this. The next letter is dated, Saturday, 6 January 1917.

My dearest darling Maggie,

Just a line telling you that I am in the best of health and spirits. Glad to hear that you and little Maggie are keeping well. Having some changeable weather, cold here today, with nice rain in the night. Always manages to rain at nights. Received your letter dated 31 December yesterday. Will answer further on. Changed PO in French post office, exchange in Francs 8.25. Came in very useful. Had a pay day, also settling up day, was five francs in credit so don't owe the army anything, so only drawed 5 Frs. Did I tell you that my watch stopped on Lord Mayor's Show Day, 9 November? Yesterday, managed to find a watchmaker after a struggle. Broke glass also broke some small works inside. Wrote to Bill and George on 4 January. They will be surprised. You never said if you received that photo yet, or Xmas card I sent you. Have you had that one (green envelope) we only have one now and again. Had a field day this week. Some doings! Lovely walk there and back. Done my first guard in this regiment this week. No complaints only too much sloping arms for my liking. Letter from Southfield's yesterday, all keeping well except of course colds, which are very fashionable in England and France. Very glad got rid of mine.

Enclosing ASC card (Plate 22), the only one I could get. Will try and get the other as soon as I can. Well dear, will now answer your welcome letter. We are still resting. No good taking notice of those at Southfield about the old chap. While he is doing that he has less to spend on bacca and beer. The money wouldn't reach Southfields. Believe he is harmless as regards to anything else. I myself would trust him for that. Daresay he will send me along some stuff one of these days. You can trust us boys for that. Let Arthur get out here and the beer talk will stop. Sorry to hear about poor Alice. It's silly of her to worry herself about him. Tell her from me, he is as safe as houses. They are some distance away. Had them behind me once. Damme noisy things. As you say, he is not like us three, in amongst it. Sugar and butter are very dear out here. Butter something about 3/- a lb, and sugar hard to get. Bread 1Fr a loaf, don't go half as far as English bread. I myself eat plenty of it. That where my money goes. Bread and candles. So, you had tea with Mrs Hampshire. What sort of house have they got? Suppose when war is over, they will want to move again. No good taking notice of Mrs Horren. He never wrote to me. Believe he is keeping well. Well my dear, very small letter for you this time. Cannot think of any more at present so must dry up with very best love and kisses and best of luck to both, from your loving husband, Horace.

X for little Maggie. P.S. Have just received small parcel. Very kind of you. Will try them and see if they are any good.

That's an intriguing postscript! Just what will he try and see if they are any good? Socks? Cold remedy? Homemade cakes? Maggie has been socialising with some other wife whose husband is at war. This husband is apparently in the artillery and a bit further behind the lines. Those noisy things, as Horace calls them. Food prices are compared with those at home. Probably to those that Horace remembers, as by this time in the war shortages were occurring of many basic foodstuffs, due to the U-boat campaign. Maggie has probably not told Horace of these. His father has been up to some mischief but nothing serious. Horace has a nice line in irony and talks of "a nice walk", to some manoeuvres that were held, and often mentions "nice rain". Imagine spending half your life living in an open trench for days on end. No rainfall could possibly be nice, nor any frosts. The humour of the British soldier has helped him to survive campaigns worldwide.

Friday, 19 January 1917
My Dearest darling Maggie,
Just a line letting you know that I am in the best of health and spirits. Have got rid of cold now. Having some dull weather now. Monday night rained very hard. Tuesday was dull and cold. Had two field days, Monday and Tuesday. Nice long walk there and back, warm us up. Went to church parade last Sunday. Have service in Picture Palace. The Parson always prays for them at home. The picture Palace is run by our division. Have not been to see them yet. Done well Sunday and Monday nights. Had two nice suppers of two fried eggs and chips, went down all right. Make a nice change of diet for us. The only chance we have to feed ourselves is when we are resting. They cost 1 Fr 2 ½ a time. Letter from Baker yesterday. Tells me they had a rough time this Xmas and still plenty of it now. They had women and soldiers there but he said they were useless. Can guess what sort of a mess they were in. (Because I wasn't there) Mr Eland is still very bad on half pay. Expect he will have to take his pension. Old pal of mine, a sorter, killed. Very sorry to hear that. He was such a nice fellow. No end of chaps sick this Xmas time, no doubt due to the foggy weather. Received a nice parcel last night from Emma, containing Mince pies, Xmas pudding, butter, tin of sausages, chocolate, nuts and cakes. Very kind of her. Must write tomorrow and thank her. No letter inside, only name outside. Gave Southfield's address. Everything arrived safe. The Mince pies were whole; they arrived just as though they just put in. The first I tasted went down all right. You can picture me and Eggleton having a feed while laying on our beds and thinking of home. Poor little Maggie, guess she cried when Johnny scratched her face. Well, that nothing for

children, in their glory when they can scratch one another's faces. Yes, CB same as in London. Makes no difference, was nothing serious. Poor Eggleton done four more days since. I had such a rotten cold and feeling out of sorts at the time. Anyhow, that over and done. Don't talk about the bath, that only a name for it. If you are lucky might get a basin full, always think of those gas times. Can't do that here. Yes, hope this year will be better than the last year for you and everybody else. Well Maggie, have told you all at present so must dry up, with very best Love and kisses and best of luck to you and little Maggie, from your loving husband, Horace.

So, yet more Field Days for the resting troops. Something coming up soon, maybe? Horace obviously enjoys the church parades and the chance to sing a few hymns. He finds it a bit unusual having the service in the Battalion cinema. So far, he hasn't sampled the programme, which would, of course, be of silent films.

Further opportunities to sample the delights of fried eggs and chips and a welcome food parcel to be shared with his good friend Eggleton. I wonder where the other two of his group are, Harradine and Lane? Both he and Eggleton have run afoul of military discipline again, for some minor infringements. All taken in the stride of the, by now, veteran soldiers. The next letter is dated, Saturday, 20 January 1917.

My dearest darling Maggie,

Just a line to tell you that I am in the best of health and spirits, hoping you and little Maggie are the same. Having some very cold weather now and plenty of snow. Last Tuesday night, we had fall of snow six inches. Very nice! We finish our rest 12 January. Been up again and back for four days. Believe shortly we are leaving this part of the line and damme good job too. Sent you letter yesterday. You will notice that they were written on Wednesday, 10 January, being no collection until yesterday the 19th. Also sent you one of our Xmas cards (Plate 22). A bit late but thought you would like one. They came from the Dardanelle's to this country.

They were selling them Xmas time, but the new year gave them away. Also sent Mother one. Just had letter from Con, has very little to say, like myself. Arthur tells me he is home for 10 days, and over he comes. Did you see him? Eggleton has gone away, how long for don't know. When we left our rest place, went to some tents, and the next day Sunday last, walked 14 miles in the snow to where we are now (full pack).

Last Friday week I done well. Papers, parcel, letter from you, one from Mother and Arthur, so I have been busy answering them. Yesterday got rid of seven of them and now have three to answer. I've done some writing since I've been out here. Will answer your letter, parcel, two lots of Mirrors and yesterday had Mirror and Postman's Gazette. Believe that all. Letter dated 5 January . No, my Xmas was two small pieces of meat and water. Lucky to get that. Was all fresh meat there, never saw any bully. Your parcel arrived Sunday before Xmas. I left Saturday before. It arrived the right time, but unfortunately, I wasn't there. Anyhow, was not wasted. Besides, they are very slack as regards post in this Regt. You can send me Bill's letter. I will return it. I wrote to him on 5 January but had no answer yet. You are too good looking to break the man's camera. Tell little Maggie I am still carrying her card with me. No, don't send me any eggs. You know I don't care for hard-boiled eggs. If they are half boiled, might smash. Very kind of you to offer to send them. Besides, water hard to get now. Always frozen. Hard job to get water to wash with. Glad to hear little Maggie done well. Hung my sock up but no luck. Will soon be school time for her. Nice job for you, to take her to school and back. Carry on the clubs as usual if you can afford to do so. Yes, my cold is better now. Your sweets arrived too late but was not wasted. Talk about going to Church and speaking about soldiers, when they speak about those at home, sometimes brings water to my eyes. One cannot help it out here. Can guess how you would be, yes when I come back. The boys done well but never mind, I was happy knowing that you and all were all right at home. Now I don't care much for cards as a rule but they are nice to receive whilst one is out in this damme country amongst the mud.

Yes, letter does just as well for me. Glad you enjoyed yourself but can quite understand your feelings, me not being there, but never mind, will be home for the next the way things are going out here. No, the contents of your parcel were not hard, anyhow, we soon got rid of them, but the chicken and ham paste was very salty. The pudding was grand, only one thing wrong with it, it was very moreish. Apples was all right, in fact all contents were all right, only the pies and cakes were in crumbs. Now, letter in parcel 7 January. Everything was all right. What O Scotts Emulsion. Nearly had a fit. Was a treat. If you keep on sending me parcels and money, I know you are only keeping yourself short, will come home and pull your nose. Knowing very well it awfully kind of you to send them, but I know very well you must be keeping yourself short as the prices of stuff is very high in London and you have enough to do to keep yourself. Your 2/- have bought me some tea and cakes in the Y.M.C.A.

The dog rolls were great, whole as though they were just packed. That what I call a treat. We cannot get those out here.

No, glad the bottle was not broken. You done the right thing drop it down the stairs. The cakes were nice. When you send me parcels always put in cakes? Cannot buy them out here and as you know makes a change. Also candles. Such a hard job to get.

Can picture little Maggie assisting you in making the cakes. Tell her for me she made them well. Expect she was covered with flour. No there is nothing I want, but you send always eatables. Forget about the Salmon, A1 for tea and supper. Now don't you keep on sending me money or else you will be for it. About that photo, sorry I overlook it in your letter. Put that down to the shells that slip past my head, and that photo slipped my eyesight. As long as you got it all right. Well Maggie have told you all I can think of, so must close with very best love and kisses to you and little Maggie and the best of luck to you. Hoping to be amongst you shortly. Give Maggie big kiss for me. Am afraid I shall have to do a lot of things when I come home tell her. Daresay her tongue will never stop. From your loving Husband, Horace.

A nice long chatty letter full of the matter-of-fact everyday happenings that Horace is experiencing. He is still moving around quite a lot, and he has temporarily lost his chum, Eggleton. A long, 14 mile walk in the snow, carrying all his equipment has brought him to a tented encampment. That he is missing his home and family goes without saying, but in little things he says it is obvious that they are never far from his thoughts and in this letter, he muses on the sort of Christmas that the rest of the family must have had. Yet still he can say, "Never mind, I was happy." But in the next sentence he speaks of "this damme country amongst the mud". He continues to worry that Maggie is leaving herself short of money in sending him food parcels but he emphasises how very eagerly he welcomes their arrival. And a little joke, he forgot to include a photograph in his previous letter "due to the shells slipping past his head". And of course, he is looking forward to coming home on leave soon. The next correspondence received by Maggie is one of the ubiquitous Field Service Postcards, pre-printed with phrases, which the sender is required to delete or leave in, as he feels appropriate. Then, a letter dated Monday, 29 January 1917.

My dearest darling Maggie,

Just a line letting you know that |I am still alive and kicking. Am in the best of health and spirits after a rough time. Having some very cold weather here now. Hell of a job to keep warm. Received your two letters and three lots of papers. Eggleton has been transferred to the RE so I am alone. Believe he has a decent job not far from us. No doubt you will see by the papers that the British have been in action. Last Saturday our Regiment was there and glad to say came out without a scratch. Should not like many more of those jobs we gave them Germans. Feeling somewhat stiff today but that will soon wear off. They didn't half bombard us with shells. Every minute I thought my last day had come but thank goodness am safe and sound, so you have no cause to worry yourself. You could picture me jumping out of the trench and running towards them. Will now answer one with no date, only

Sunday night. Sorry to hear about little Maggie having a cold, but by your second letter she is all right again. Yes, my love, I know you will do anything for me. Have not managed to get other cards yet, glad you liked them. All that money from post office must be back pay on overtime. Came as a gift to you. Machine is just the article you require, so you are landed now and you will be able to amuse yourself now. That's a bargain. Don't worry about the money. You can do whatever you like with your own money. Yes, you are right, machine is ten times better than War Loan. Tell them I am giving years of my life to them, also losing money while being out in this damme country fighting. Don't worry about saving. Have all you want. What Club Widows do you mean? The Wandsworth? If so, keep on paying until I come home. Couldn't get my watch mended after all. These French people are humbugging lot. Took the watch out of his hand. Yes, it's the rough use they have what with falling about and etc. Cannot wonder at it. In our platoon about a dozen watches are broke. By the way I mention your name in Mother's letter, just to please them. Don't see any reason why I should because they are always seeing you. Ought to know more about you than I do. Very nice PC from Maggie. Daresay she was highly delighted. Letter dated 24 January received yesterday when I came back from trenches. Glad you both are keeping well. Wrote you two letters last week, one green envelope. No letters collected since last Wednesday. Will look out for that parcel, also bacon in pastry, won't we have a feed. Can quite picture Maggie's cake. So, they came for the Rabbit at last. That a good job. Yes, I wrote to him and had answer last week. Tell Mr Taylor will write to him shortly, we don't get much time for writing here. Have received no fags from him yet. Daresay somebody enjoying them. Sorry to hear you are having some rotten weather. I often wish you were out here to keep my back warm in bed. Yes, I will take great care of myself, leave all that to me. I don't want to see another winter out here. If a man can stick it, he can stick anything. It awful here, snow on the ground and freezing hard you can guess how it is. You look all right in trousers, take no notice of them. If they want you to sell some of our home, tell them to inform me. I am giving my life to them, that's enough for them. Don't you part with anything or do anything. You have quite enough to do. Heard all about that explosion. Must have been awful nearby. Tell little Maggie I have been fighting the Germans. What with shooting and bombing them in their dugouts we give them hot time. So, she will have something to say now. Of course, we never all come back. Our lot lost all officers, Sergt Major, Quarter Master, and NCO. It was awful. It all right if one keeps up his spirits. I went neck or nothing and came out trumps. Well, my dear, my fingers are so sore can hardly write so will dry up with very best love and kisses and the best of luck, from your loving Husband, Horace. X for little Maggie.

Despite his attempts to gloss over things and keep the letter on subjects from home, it is painfully obvious the Horace has been through a very traumatic few days. Military history reports that the middle of January 1917 was bitterly cold, and by 14 January the ground was sufficiently hardened for the Generals to contemplate further attacks but a short spell of warmer weather brought chaos again. It froze the water holes and forced the men to melt ice from shell holes. The British are recorded as having made three raids at this time, two of which were successful. And while all this is going on in France, Maggie is being harassed back home to sell some of her possessions, probably because she had applied for a little government assistance, which was Means Tested. Horace, on hearing of this is naturally angry and orders her not to sell anything. And, in what now seems to be a prophetic sentence, says, "Tell them I am giving my life for them." Because Maggie's next letter to Horace is returned, marked "Unable to Deliver". Then in an official letter, dated 26 February 1917 is given the dreadful news her husband, Rifleman Horace Surtees has been killed in Action on 30 January.

Plate 18. "Little Maggie". Miss Maggie Dora Surtees.
Born 1912 Died 1989.

Over the next three years, Maggie was to write many letters to the war office, and to people who might have been with or might have known Horace. Despite all her efforts she was unable to find out how he was killed or where he was buried. A letter from a young lady who was engaged to another soldier in the regiment says that Horace was killed near Bapaume but there was no grave. A letter came from Horace's good friend, Eggleton, which sheds some light on what happened.

Dated 21/3/17.

Dear Mrs Surtees,

I am sorry to have kept you waiting such a long time for news of poor Horace's death but I did not get an answer until last night, but it was too late to write then so I am writing this early today to try and catch the post. It happened at night, two days after they made an attack. According to Lane's letter they, Horace and another young chap, were sitting in a small dugout asleep when the shell came over and burst. It killed them both instantly. He could not have suffered any pain, for as Lane says in his letter, the concussion killed them both before any shrapnel hit them. All this is very poor consolation to you I know but under the circumstances, it was the easiest death for he felt nothing of it at all. Poor old chap, it has been a very hard blow to you and I hope you are bearing it as bravely as possible. Mr Lane sends his sympathies to you and Mr Harradine is writing to you and he may explain the case more fully as he was not more than 100 yards way. Well Mrs Surtees, I do not think there is anything more that I can do now but if there is anything else you want to know write and tell me and I will do my best to find out for you. Trusting this will find both you and your little daughter in the best of health I will close with my Best wishes for the future, your sincere friend, J. Eggleton.

Despite all Maggie's efforts in writing to other friends in the platoon and to the unit Padre, the War office, and many others, Horace's grave, if indeed he ever had one, was never found. He is listed on the Memorial at Thiepval, on the Somme, which bears the names of over 73,000 British and Commonwealth men who have no known grave and who fell on the Somme between July 1916 and 20 March 1918. 141 feet high, it was designed by Sir Edwin Lutyens and has 16 piers on whose faces the names of the Missing are inscribed.

The name of Rifleman Surtees. H. appears on pier 5 face B, among the City of London Rifles, attached to Inniskilling Fusiliers.

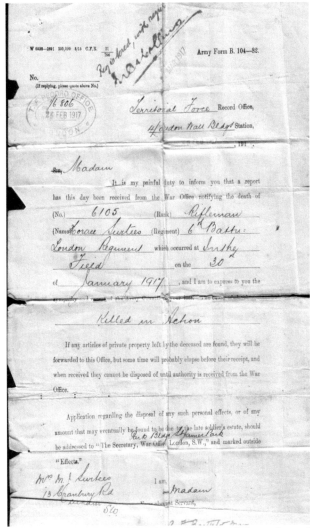

Plate 18. Official notification of the death in action of Rifleman H. Surtees.

On 21 June 1920, the South-Western District of the post office held a service to unveil and dedicate the staff memorial. Led by the Venerable the Archdeacon of Middlesex, with the Chairman of the District, the unveiling was carried out by Mr Charles C. Sanderson, Controller London Postal Services. Among those listed as having given their lives for their King and Country is, Rifleman Horace Surtees, City of London Rifles, a Postman.

Plate 20. The THIEPVAL Memorial to The Missing of the Somme. Bears the names of over 77,000 British and Commonwealth men who have no known grave.